MINDFULNESS FOR BEGINNERS

2025

A Simple Guide to Achieve Inner Peace and Mental Clarity

Alex C. Wei

Dedication

This book is dedicated to those who seek peace in a chaotic world. May you find calmness and clarity through the simple yet transformative practice of mindfulness.

Content

Introduction...7

  Chapter 1: What is Mindfulness?.........................9

    Understanding Mindfulness................................9

    Why Mindfulness Matters.............................. 10

    Mindfulness is for Everyone.......................... 11

  Chapter 2: Simple Breathing Techniques for Calmness...13

    How to Practice Mindful Breathing...............13

    Why It Works..14

  Chapter 3: Body Scan for Stress Relief............... 15

    How to Perform a Body Scan........................ 15

    The Benefits...16

  Chapter 4: Mindful Observation: Cultivating Awareness.. 17

    A Simple Exercise in Observation...................17

  Chapter 5: Practicing Gratitude Through Mindfulness.. 19

    A Daily Gratitude Practice............................ 19

    How Gratitude Enhances Mindfulness..........20

  Chapter 6: Applying Mindfulness in Everyday Life.. 21

    Mindful Eating...21

    Mindful Walking..22

    Building a Mindful Routine..........................22

Conclusion.. 25

Introduction

Mindfulness is a powerful tool for navigating the stresses of modern life. In our fast-paced world, it's easy to get lost in the constant noise of responsibilities, worries, and distractions. ***"Mindfulness for Beginners 2025"*** is designed to offer a simple and accessible guide to practicing mindfulness in daily life, helping you find inner peace and mental clarity.

This short guide will introduce you to the core concepts and practical steps to incorporate mindfulness into your routine, whether you're at home, at work, or on the go. It's perfect for those who are just starting out or for anyone looking to refresh their understanding of mindfulness. The techniques shared in this book are easy to follow and can be practiced by anyone, regardless of age or experience.

Chapter 1: What is Mindfulness?

In today's fast-paced world, it's easy to get caught up in the whirlwind of daily life. We often find ourselves dwelling on the past or worrying about the future, which leads to stress, anxiety, and a lack of focus. Mindfulness is the practice of bringing our attention to the present moment, intentionally and without judgment. It allows us to experience life as it unfolds, moment by moment, helping us break free from the mental clutter that weighs us down.

Understanding Mindfulness

At its core, mindfulness is about paying attention to what's happening right now. It's the art of being fully aware of your thoughts, feelings, and surroundings without getting overwhelmed by them. Whether you're eating, walking, or simply breathing, mindfulness helps you stay connected to the present.

Think of it as training your mind to focus on the here and now instead of being distracted by worries or regrets. The more we practice mindfulness, the better we become at managing stress and finding mental clarity, even in challenging situations.

Why Mindfulness Matters

Research shows that practicing mindfulness can reduce stress, improve focus, and enhance emotional well-being. When we are mindful, we can respond to life's challenges more calmly and effectively. It's like pressing pause on life's chaos and giving ourselves the chance to reset.

By practicing mindfulness, you can:

- Reduce anxiety and stress
- Improve concentration and focus
- Gain a deeper understanding of your thoughts and emotions
- Cultivate a sense of peace and balance

Mindfulness is for Everyone

The best part about mindfulness is that it's simple and accessible to everyone. You don't need any special equipment or extensive training to get started. All you need is a willingness to be present and to practice regularly, even if it's just for a few minutes each day.

In the next chapter, we'll explore a basic breathing exercise that will help you start your mindfulness journey, allowing you to center yourself and achieve inner calm, no matter where you are.

Chapter 2: Simple Breathing Techniques for Calmness

Breathing is something we do every second of every day, but how often do we pay attention to it? One of the simplest and most effective ways to start practicing mindfulness is by focusing on your breath. Mindful breathing helps bring your attention to the present moment and calms your mind and body.

How to Practice Mindful Breathing

1. **Find a quiet place** where you won't be disturbed. Sit comfortably with your back straight.
2. **Close your eyes** and take a deep breath through your nose, feeling your lungs fill up.
3. **Slowly exhale** through your mouth, focusing on the sensation of your breath leaving your body.

4. **Continue this cycle** of slow, deep breathing. If your mind starts to wander, gently bring your attention back to your breath.

This exercise can be done anywhere—at home, at work, or even in the middle of a busy day. Just a few minutes of mindful breathing can reduce stress and help you regain focus.

Why It Works

Focusing on your breath helps quiet the mental chatter that often leads to anxiety or overwhelm. It grounds you in the present, allowing you to let go of distractions and find calmness, even in stressful situations.

Chapter 3: Body Scan for Stress Relief

The body scan is another simple mindfulness technique that helps you reconnect with your physical sensations. When we're stressed, we often carry tension in our bodies without even realizing it. A body scan helps you release that tension and bring your mind back to the present.

How to Perform a Body Scan

1. **Lie down or sit comfortably**, ensuring your body is fully supported.
2. **Close your eyes** and take a few deep breaths.
3. **Start at your toes**, bringing your full attention to how they feel. Are they tense? Relaxed? Just notice without judgment.
4. Slowly **move your attention up your body**, focusing on your feet, legs, abdomen, chest, shoulders, arms, and head.

5. **As you notice tension**, breathe into that area and consciously relax it before moving to the next part of your body.

The Benefits

By scanning your body, you'll become more aware of where you hold tension and how to release it. This simple practice helps reduce stress and improves your ability to relax, promoting a sense of inner peace.

Chapter 4: Mindful Observation: Cultivating Awareness

Mindful observation is a way to engage with your surroundings more fully. It encourages you to focus on what you can see, hear, or feel in the present moment, making it a great tool for reducing anxiety and staying grounded.

A Simple Exercise in Observation

1. **Choose an object** in your environment (a tree, a flower, or even a cup of coffee).
2. **Focus your attention** entirely on that object. Notice its color, shape, texture, and any other details.
3. **Observe without judgment**. If your mind starts to wander, gently bring it back to the object.

This exercise can be done anywhere. By practicing mindful observation, you'll develop a heightened awareness of your surroundings, which can help you stay present and reduce feelings of overwhelm.

Chapter 5: Practicing Gratitude Through Mindfulness

Gratitude and mindfulness go hand in hand. When we practice mindfulness, we become more aware of the positive things in our lives, and expressing gratitude can enhance this awareness.

A Daily Gratitude Practice

1. At the end of each day, **take a moment to reflect** on three things you are grateful for. They can be small or big—anything that makes you feel positive.
2. As you think about each one, **focus on the feeling of gratitude** and allow yourself to fully experience that emotion.
3. Write these things down or simply reflect on them in your mind.

How Gratitude Enhances Mindfulness

Practicing gratitude shifts your focus from what's lacking to what's present in your life. It encourages you to appreciate the moment, which is at the core of mindfulness.

Chapter 6: Applying Mindfulness in Everyday Life

Mindfulness isn't just something you do in meditation—it's something you can bring into every part of your day. Whether you're eating, walking, or working, mindfulness can help you stay focused and grounded.

Mindful Eating

The next time you eat, try this:

1. **Sit down and focus** on your food. Notice its colors, textures, and smells.
2. **Take small bites** and chew slowly, paying attention to the taste and how the food feels in your mouth.
3. **Avoid distractions**, like your phone or TV, while you eat.

Mindful Walking

As you walk, focus on the movement of your body:

1. **Notice your feet** hitting the ground and how your body shifts with each step.
2. **Tune into your surroundings**, paying attention to the sights and sounds around you.
3. **Walk slowly and with intention**, fully experiencing each step.

Building a Mindful Routine

Start by incorporating mindfulness into simple, daily activities—like brushing your teeth or making your bed. The more you practice, the easier it becomes to stay present throughout your day. Mindfulness is about being aware of the moment, and when practiced regularly, it can lead to greater peace, clarity, and balance in your life.

By following these simple, step-by-step practices, you can begin to integrate mindfulness into your life with ease, making it a tool you can rely on to achieve both mental clarity and inner peace.

Conclusion

Mindfulness is a simple yet profound practice that can transform your life by helping you become more present, calm, and focused. Through the exercises in this short guide—breathing techniques, body scans, mindful observation, and gratitude—you now have the tools to cultivate mindfulness in your daily routine. By taking just a few moments each day to center yourself, you can reduce stress, improve your mental clarity, and enjoy a deeper sense of peace.

Remember, mindfulness is not about perfection; it's about progress. As you continue your journey, be patient with yourself. Every small step you take brings you closer to a more balanced and peaceful life. Let mindfulness be your guide in navigating the challenges of everyday life with clarity and compassion.